SAUSAGE

Paul Stewart

Illustrated by
Nick Ward

OXFORD
UNIVERSITY PRESS

OXFORD
UNIVERSITY PRESS

Great Clarendon Street, Oxford OX2 6DP

Oxford University Press is a department of the University of Oxford.
It furthers the University's objective of excellence in research, scholarship,
and education by publishing worldwide in

Oxford New York

Auckland Bangkok Buenos Aires Cape Town Chennai
Dar es Salaam Delhi Hong Kong Istanbul Karachi Kolkata
Kuala Lumpur Madrid Melbourne Mexico City Mumbai Nairobi
São Paulo Shanghai Taipei Tokyo Toronto

with an associated company in Berlin

Oxford is a registered trade mark of Oxford University Press
in the UK and in certain other countries

British Library Cataloguing in Publication Data

Data available

ISBN 0 19 919488 2

3 5 7 9 10 8 6 4 2

Guided Reading Pack (6 of the same title): ISBN 0 19 919568 4
Mixed Pack (1 of 6 different titles): ISBN 0 19 919491 2
Class Pack (6 copies of 6 titles): ISBN 0 19 919492 0

Printed in Hong Kong

For Anna

Contents

Chapter 1
A Brilliant Idea

"What *am* I going to do?" said Ella.
"It's eleven o'clock, already!"

She was at the park with her dog, Sausage. It was where she always went when she had a problem.

The School Fair started at one, and Ella still didn't know what to go in for. The talent competition? The painting competition? Fancy dress?

"Woof! Woof!" Sausage barked.

All of a sudden, Ella was struck by a brilliant idea. Of course! Why hadn't she thought of it before? The Dog Competition!

She looked round. Sausage, still barking loudly, was racing off towards a muddy puddle.

"Come here, Sausage," Ella called.

"And miss that wonderful mud?" thought Sausage. "You must be joking."

"Sausage!" shouted Ella. She chased after him. "You've got to look your best this afternoon. There's a dog compe —"

Too late. Sausage had jumped into
the puddle and he was already rolling
in thick mud.

"— tition," said Ella. She sighed.
"Now I'll have to give you a bath."

"Nonsense," thought Sausage.

"If I splash about a bit, I'll
end up as clean as anything. Anyway,
I don't want to go in for a stupid dog-
comp-a ... comp-a-tishoo ..."

"Sausage!" bellowed Ella.

Sausage turned. Ella looked cross, and he hated that. He trotted over to her. "Don't be upset," he thought.

He jumped up to give her a big slurpy kiss.

"Yuk!" Ella shouted out. "Get down, Sausage!"

Sausage cocked his head and stared at Ella, puzzled. There were black marks all down her T-shirt and jeans. Sometimes she could be so messy!

"If we *are* going to win that comp-a-tishoo," he thought, "then *you'll* have to look your best, too."

Chapter 2
Sausage

Sausage hadn't always been called
Sausage. A year ago, Mum and Dad
had taken Ella to the local dogs' home.
Ella and the puppy had looked at each
other, and it was love at first sight.

"He's the one I want," said Ella. "I'll
call him Sebastian."

Time passed, and Sebastian grew –
or rather, most of him did.

*   *   *

For though he had a proud head, powerful body, and a long tail, Sebastian's legs remained stubby and short.

"He looks like a barrel on four sticks," said Dad.

"Don't," said Ella. "You'll hurt his feelings."

"Well, he does," Dad said.

"Something's not right."

Mum phoned the dogs' home and discovered that yes, Sebastian was a mixture. His father was a Labrador, but his mother was – a dachshund.

"A sausage dog!" Dad exclaimed. And the name stuck. From that moment on, Sebastian was Sausage.

*　　　*　　　*

"Good dog," Ella murmured, as she rubbed Sausage's clean wet fur with a towel. "You look lovely." She tickled his ears. "We'll win that Dog Competition for sure – as long as you're a good dog."

Sausage wagged his tail. When Ella was happy, he was happy.

"Good dog?" he thought, "I'm going to be the *best* dog! You'll see."

Chapter 3
Something Delicious

Ready at last, Ella and Sausage left the house. Outside the school, other dogs were arriving with their owners. Sausage knew the dogs from the park. Ella knew the children from school.

There was Tyrone, a pudgy, short-haired bulldog with a pudgy, short-haired bully called Luke.

There was Beth, a scatty spaniel with a scatty girl called Lisa.

And there was Scamp, a scruffy terrier with a scruffy boy called Terry.

Sausage turned to Ella. Did *they* look alike? Certainly, they both had sandy hair and brown eyes. But if Ella was really to look like him, then she would have to walk along on her knees.

Just then, Mrs Everett the school

secretary appeared with her tiny
poodle, Mimi. Now, they *did* look like
each other!

Sausage sniffed. "Silly creature," he
thought, "and as for Mimi, she's a
disgrace to all dogs!"

The School Fair was in full swing as
Ella and Sausage picked their way
through the crowds. Sausage was in
a hurry.

He'd smelled something delicious
and he tugged Ella around the fair
until he found it.

A hot dog stall!

"Yum," said Ella. She counted
her money.

"Pity," she said. "I'd love one, but
I've only just got enough money for
the Dog Competition."

"That's all right," thought Sausage.
"I'll get you one."

He was about to jump up and seize
the nearest hot dog in his mouth,
when Ella tugged his lead.

"Come on, Sausage," she said.
Sausage tugged back.
"Sausage!" said Ella, sharply.
He stopped pulling.
"Spoilsport," he whined.

Just then, a voice crackled over the loudspeaker: "Will all dog owners please make their way to the school field. This is the last call for the Dog Competition."

Chapter 4
Jump, Fetch, and Stay

In the field, Ella entered Sausage for the competition. He was given a number. Number thirteen. Ella hoped it wasn't unlucky thirteen!

"Be good," she told Sausage, as they took their place at the end of the line.

"Of course," thought Sausage. He glanced at the other dogs. "Anything they can do, I can do *much* better!"

A woman with "Judge" pinned to her jacket stood up. "Good afternoon," she said. "I see you all have lovely dogs. But there can be only one winner of the cup and cash prize. We are about to find out who that is."

"Me, of course," thought Sausage.

"The competition is divided into three parts," the judge went on. "Jump, Fetch, and Stay. The first part will take place over here." She pointed to a series of numbered gates. "Competitor number one, please."

Lisa led Beth forwards. The jumping began.

Beth quickly jumped over the gates in the right order.

"She's very good," said Ella.

"Humph!" thought Sausage. "Boring! I can do far better than that."

At last, it was Sausage's turn. Ella pointed to the first gate.

"Jump, boy," she said.

"With *my* legs?" thought Sausage.
"Not likely." He had planned a special
routine all of his own.

He scurried under gate number one,
skidded round gates two, three and
four in a neat snaking movement, then
through gate five.

Already he could hear the crowd
laughing. They loved him!

And the best bit was still to come.
With a joyful bark, he jumped over
gate six, up on to gate seven, where he
balanced for a moment.

Then he threw himself into Ella's
waiting arms.

"Ta-da!"

Ella put Sausage on to the ground.
Her head was pounding. Her face
was red.

"He did manage one jump," said the
judge, kindly.

"Yes," thought Sausage, proudly. "On
top of everything else, I even managed
a jump. We're bound to win!"

The second event – Fetch – tested
how well and how fast the dogs could
bring things back. Once again, the
other dogs did just as they were told.

But Sausage had decided to make
the tricks more interesting.

"Number thirteen," the judge said
at last.

Ella and Sausage stepped forwards
to the sound of laughter and whistles.
"It's that funny dog with the short
legs," someone said.

Sausage bowed. "I'm going to enjoy
this," he thought.

For the first trick, Sausage was
supposed to run and fetch a rubber
ring when Ella gave the command.
He got ready. He got set.

Ella raised her arm and tossed the ring across the field. "Fet ... " she began. But Sausage was already dashing after it.

"I'll show them," he thought. "Any fool can carry a ring in their mouth. I shall return with it balanced on my nose."

As the ring rolled along the ground, Sausage thrust in his nose...

... and got it stuck fast.

"Whoops," thought Sausage. He tried to get it off – with his front paws, his back leg, and by spinning round and round.

But the ring wouldn't budge.

The crowd went wild.

"Here, boy," he heard Ella calling. "Come HERE!"

"Hang on," he thought. "If I can just ... "

The next instant, Ella yanked the ring roughly from his nose. "I thought I told you to be good, Sausage," she hissed. "Everyone's laughing at us."

Sausage paused. "Are you sure?" he thought, uneasily.

He looked round at the sea of faces.
They were jeering and pointing. Ella
was right. They *were* laughing at him.
He hung his head. He had made a fool
of himself – and Ella.

Again!

He remembered the time he'd got stuck in the swing bin. The time he'd dug a hole in the garden so deep he couldn't get out. And that awful day when he'd got trapped inside the pipe that workmen were laying at the front of the house. It had taken three hours to pull him free.

But this time, he'd really gone too far. Ella was crying.

"I'm sorry, Ella," he thought. "What can I do to cheer you up?" His nose twitched. Of course! He knew exactly what to do.

"Sausage!" Ella called through her tears, as he bounded across the grass. "Where are you going now?"

The crowd laughed louder than ever. Ella stood there, wishing the ground would swallow her up.

"Here he comes again!" someone shouted a moment later. "Look at him go!"

Back in the field, Sausage dashed over to Ella and dropped something on to the grass.

He stood there, tail wagging. Ella looked down. A hot dog lay at her feet.

"It's for you," thought Sausage. "A present – to cheer you up."

Ella was furious. "Come on, Sausage!" she said, and grasped him by the collar. "First, I've got to say sorry for that hot dog you stole. Then, we're going home."

"Home?" thought Sausage. "We can't go home." He sat down. "We haven't won the comp-a-tishoo yet."

"Come on!" said Ella, pulling him with all her strength.

But Sausage would not budge.

"You are HOPELESS!" Ella shouted.
She kicked the hot dog, angrily.

"What a waste!" thought Sausage,
sadly. "What was wrong with it,
anyway?"

He watched the hot dog bounce
over the grass ...

Chapter 5

Control Your Dogs!

It landed close to Beth. She was about to tuck in to the delicious treat which had appeared from nowhere, when Tyrone snapped at it.

But Scamp wanted the hot dog, too. He leapt on to the bulldog's back and bit his ear. Tyrone yelped with pain and snarled at Mimi.

"Keep that horrible dog away from my Mimikins!" Mrs Everett squealed. She hit out with her umbrella.

Scamp spotted his chance, snatched the hot dog, and swallowed it in one great, greedy gulp.

All at once, the field exploded with frantic barking. Twelve of the thirteen dogs in the competition ran riot – and no one could stop them.

A beagle leapt at a greyhound. Two shaggy dogs – one black and one white – began chasing a Pekinese.

A Dalmatian dashed through everyone's legs, tripping them up. The crowd whooped and cheered. This was even better than the funny short-legged dog.

"Control your dogs!" the judge
bellowed.
"Jasper!"
"Beth!"
"Scamp!"
"Fred!"
"Tyrone!"

Ella was the only one not shouting.
For once, Sausage was as good as gold.
"Dreadful behaviour," he sniffed.
"You wouldn't catch me being so ..."
There was an ear-splitting yell.

The judge had raced over to control
the dogs and they had tripped her up.
Excitedly, they all piled on top
of her and licked her with their long
slobbery tongues.

"Gerroff!" she roared. "Ugh! Stop that!"

Ella couldn't stand by a moment longer. "STAY!" she told Sausage, sternly.

Sausage saw that she meant it. "Okay," he thought.

Ella marched across the grass and began pulling the dogs off the judge.

The judge scrambled to her feet. She looked furious.

"Never, in twenty-five years," she said, fiercely, "have I seen anything like it. You're all out of the competition!"

"But ... " Ella began.

"Not you, my dear," the judge said, smiling. She pointed at Sausage, who was still waiting for Ella. "The winner of this afternoon's competition is number thirteen. Sausage."

She turned to Ella. "Well done!"

Ella could hardly believe her ears. They'd won! Still dazed, she returned to Sausage, proudly carrying the winner's silver cup and a crisp ten-pound note.

"We won," she said, weakly.

"Of course we did," thought Sausage, glad to see Ella looking happy once more. "Didn't I tell you?"

"Come on, Sausage," said Ella. "Let's *both* have a hot dog. We've earned it."

About the author

I live near the sea with my wife, my son and my daughter, Anna.

Last summer, we were all picnicking on the beach when a strange-looking dog appeared from nowhere, grabbed our Frisbee and ran off. Back home, Anna persuaded me to write a story about a naughty, strange-looking - but rather sweet - dog.

Sausage is that dog!